Scholastic Children's Books,
Euston House, 24 Eversholt Street,
London, NW1 1DB, UK

A division of Scholastic Ltd
London ~ New York ~ Toronto ~ Sydney ~ Auckland
Mexico City ~ New Delhi ~ Hong Kong

Published by Scholastic Ltd, 2014

HORRIBLE HISTORIES

ANNUAL 2015

TERRY DEARY ✦ MARTIN BROWN

SCHOLASTIC

CONTENTS

This Horrible Annual belongs to:

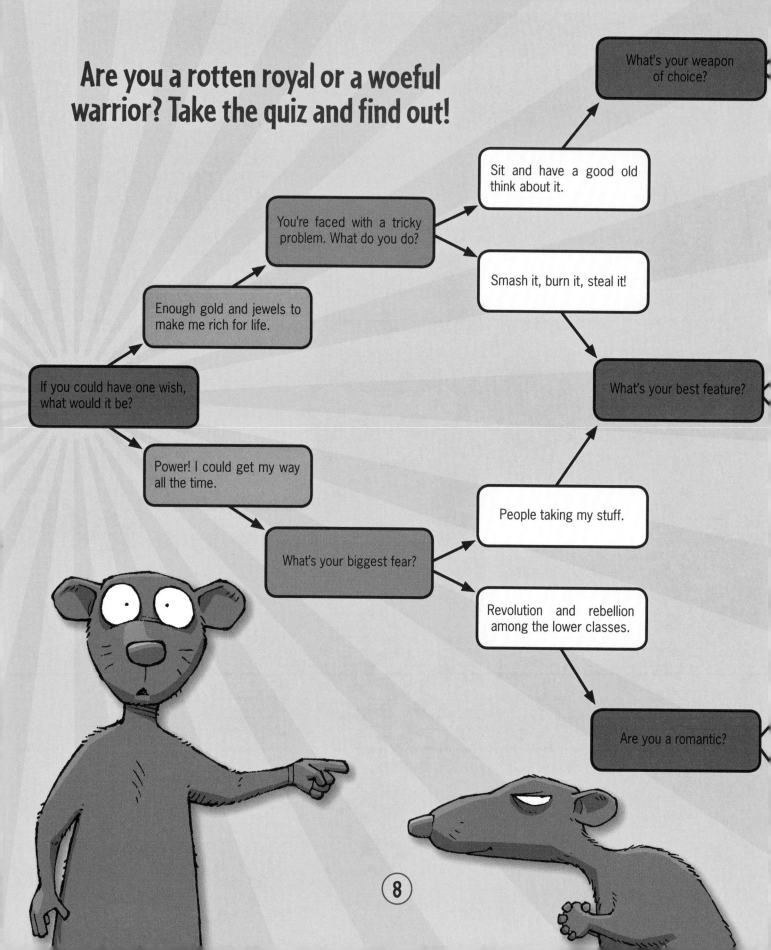

WHICH HORRIBLE HISTORIES CHARACTER ARE YOU?

Are you a rotten royal or a woeful warrior? Take the quiz and find out!

What's your weapon of choice?

Sit and have a good old think about it.

You're faced with a tricky problem. What do you do?

Smash it, burn it, steal it!

Enough gold and jewels to make me rich for life.

If you could have one wish, what would it be?

What's your best feature?

Power! I could get my way all the time.

People taking my stuff.

What's your biggest fear?

Revolution and rebellion among the lower classes.

Are you a romantic?

My razor-sharp mind and way with words. Has no one ever told you the pen is mightier than the sword?

You're WILLIAM SHAKESPEARE

You're the most famous playwright in history with a taste for truly gory stories. Some of the most horrible things to happen in your plays include eyes being ripped out on stage, live bears chasing people, mass murder and even cannibalism.

Swish, splat! You just can't beat a trusty axe.

You're THE EXECUTIONER

You're employed to chop the heads off lawbreakers and criminals. You've got a strong arm and a strong stomach, and you're not known for being particularly chatty! In fact, you've got a real air of mystery about you – dressed all in black and with a hood and mask over your face. Even your name is kept secret so no one will know you who are.

Long hair the colour of fire.

You're BOUDICA

Wow! It's not wise to get you angry. You're a Celtic queen who fought back hard when the Romans tried to take your land. You attack Roman settlements, burning them to the ground. One day you're finally defeated by a Roman general and you poison yourself.

A beard that makes me look extra fearsome.

You're A VICIOUS VIKING

You're brave, skilled with weapons and with a thirst for conquest. Very little scares you, and you'll go to any lengths to get what you want, even if it means stealing or killing. You've got a softer side too though, and you're great at carving and ship building.

Good grief no! I'm far too busy and important for such soppy things.

You're ELIZABETH I

You might be remembered today as the queen of a 'golden age', but you don't half have a bad temper. You hate to lose at anything and you make up nasty nicknames for your servants and courtiers. You never get married, and your death marks the end of the terrifying Tudors.

Yes, I fall in love all the time!

You're HENRY VIII

You're a powerful ruler with an enormous appetite – for power, for food and for wives for that matter! You have six wives during your lifetime, and a nasty habit of divorcing them or having their heads cut off! The only thing bigger than your heart is your belly.

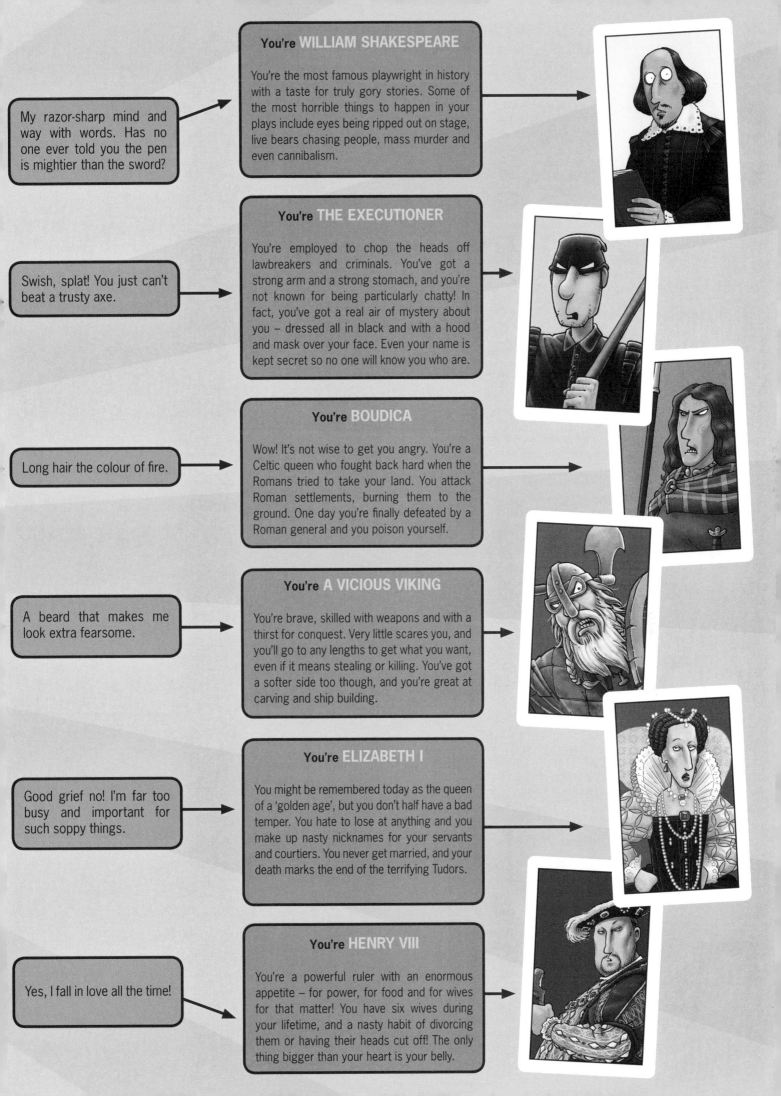

ROMAN EMPIRE QUIZ

The past was dirty and dangerous, cruel and smelly. Food was terrible and loos were lousy. It was pitiful for peasants in past times while the posh usually had it rather better. But in the dangerous days of the Roman Empire it was the emperors and the Roman nobility who had a lousy life. But how much do you know about the Romans? The empire that killed people for 'sport' then had the cheek to call the rest of the world 'barbarian'. Try this quiz ...

1 The first emperor, Augustus (63 BC – AD 14), survived longer than most. Gus's top tip for living was ...
a) He wore armour under his toga
b) He had a trained wolf by his side at all times
c) He conveniently fell ill before a battle and bottled

2 Tiberius (42 BC – AD 37) was not a sociable man and exiled himself from Rome for most of his reign. What did he say that exemplifies his attitude ...
a) 'I don't care if they hate me so long as they respect me'
b) 'Start every day off with a smile and get it over with'
c) 'Rome is a city of necks just waiting for me to chop'

3 Nero (AD 37 – 68) lit his palace gardens with the original 'Roman Candles'. What were they?
a) Fireworks imported from China
b) Ropes dipped in sheep fat
c) Christian martyrs dipped in tar

4 Emperor Galba (3 BC – AD 69) at 71 years met rival Otho and bared his neck saying, 'Strike, if it be for the good of the Romans!' His head was lopped off. Then what happened to it?
a) Otho's followers played football with it
b) It was mummified and worshipped in the Temple of the Dead Head
c) It was fed to the palace guard dogs

5 Hadrian (AD 76 – 138) famously built a wall across the north of England. One Scottish tribe to the north, the Attacotti, had a reputation for what?
a) Holding the first Scottish Olympics – featuring sword dancing, caber-tossing, tartan weaving and naked wrestling
b) Cannibalism – raiding farms and preferring to eat the shepherd rather than his sheep
c) Inventing Scottish cuisine – including haggis, kippers and marmalade

6 Marcus Aurelius (AD 121 – 180) consulted a fortune teller before a battle who said a great victory would ensue if Marcus performed an act. (The Romans lost and the fortune teller said, 'I didn't say WHO would win the great victory'.) What act did Marcus perform?
a) He threw two Christians to the lions
b) He threw two lions in the River Tiber
c) He threw two Christians in the River Tiber

7 Commodus (AD 161 – 192) gathered a group of Roman men and killed them with blows from a club, pretending they were giants. What distinguished these men?
a) They had all lost their feet from disease or accident
b) They were all found guilty of plotting to kill Commodus
c) They were all guilty of infringing Roman traffic regulations by parking chariots in a way that obstructed the highway

8 Commodus inscribed a list on a wax tablet; a list of the people he had decided (on a whim) to execute. How did that list lead to his death?
a) His mistress Marcia found it, saw her name on it and had the emperor murdered before he could execute her
b) The tablet fell on the fire, Commodus's toga caught alight and burned him to death
c) He signed it 'Emperor Commodus'. The executioner read the list, saw his name and executed him in a misunderstanding

9 Didius Julianus (AD 137 – 193) ruled for just nine weeks before being chopped by a palace guard. But how had he been appointed emperor?
a) He was the youngest of three sons of the previous emperor but murdered his two older brothers
b) He fought in single combat with the previous emperor and defeated him
c) He was the highest bidder in an auction for the imperial throne

10 Elagabalus, (AD 203 – 222), the oddest emperor of all, knew assassins were coming. He hid where he knew they'd never find him ... but they did. Where?
a) In the empress's wardrobe, covered in her highness's 173 pairs of shoes
b) In the dog kennels, covered in the skin of a dead dog
c) In a palace toilet, hidden inside a chest

Answers: 1c), 2a), 3c), 4a), 5b), 6b), 7a), 8a), 9c), 10c)

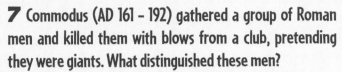

ROTTEN ROMAN GAMES
5,000 beasts were killed in one day in AD 80 in the Colosseum of Rome.

I THINK IT'S FULL

THE UNUSUAL SUSPECTS

Happy to sit at
a round table
(or under it)

Chop chop,
you don't want
to lose your
head

You'll need a
mammoth brain
to work this
one out

SPOT THE LOT

Can you spot all 10 differences?

CRUEL CRUSADES
PALESTINE, AD 1097

KNIGHTS KILLED OTHER KNIGHTS. THEN THE HEAD OF THE CHRISTIAN CHURCH - THE POPE - SAID, 'THAT IS WICKED. YOU WILL GO TO HELL. IF YOU HAVE TO KILL SOMEBODY THEN KILL PEOPLE WHO AREN'T CHRISTIANS. THAT WAY YOU WILL GO TO HEAVEN WHEN YOU DIE. GO OFF AND KILL THE MUSLIMS WHO ARE LIVING IN OUR HOLY LAND.' AND THE KNIGHTS OF EUROPE WERE HAPPY TO DO THAT. THEY SET OFF ON 'CRUSADES'.

THE TURKS CUT OPEN THE BELLIES OF CHRISTIANS THAT THEY WANT TO TORMENT WITH A LOATHSOME DEATH. THEY TEAR OUT THEIR ORGANS AND TIE THEM TO A STAKE. THEY DRAG THEIR VICTIMS ROUND THE STAKE AND FLOG THEM. THEY KILL THEM AS THEY LIE FLAT ON THE GROUND WITH THEIR GUTS OUT

IN 1095 POPE URBAN II DECIDED IT WAS TIME THE CHRISTIANS TOOK OVER JERUSALEM FOR THE CHRISTIAN CHURCH.

WE DON'T HAVE AN EXCUSE TO INVADE THE HOLY LAND, POPE URBAN

GATHER THE BEST KNIGHTS TOGETHER AND I'LL THINK OF SOMETHING

URBAN TRIED THE USUAL WAR-MAKER'S TRICK OF TELLING HIS PEOPLE HOW CRUEL THE ENEMY COULD BE.

I FEEL ANGRY

I FEEL PR

I FEEL SICK

HIGH-SPEED HISTORY

OF COURSE AN ARMY OF KNIGHTS WOULD DO MUCH BETTER ... OR WOULD THEY? THEY SET OFF ON SHIPS AND OVER LAND AND ARRIVED AT ANTIOCH BY 1097...

CONSTANTINOPLE

ROME

ANTIOC

THEY DIDN'T HAVE ENOUGH MEN TO ATTACK THE LARGE CITY SO THE TOP KNIGHT, BOHEMOND, NEEDED A SNEAKY PLAN.

I NEED A SNEAKY PLAN

WHY NOT PAY ONE OF THE GUARDS TO LEAVE A GATE OPEN?

I'VE DECIDED ... TO PAY ONE OF THE GUARDS TO LEAVE A GATE OPEN

GREAT IDEA, MY LORD!

HAH! HE WANTS A SNEAKY PLAN, NOT A STUPID PLAN.

3
BUT BOHEMOND FORGOT SOMETHING...
EXCUSE ME SIR, BUT THERE'S NO FOOD IN THE CITY. THE PEOPLE ATE IT ALL
GO OUT AND GET SOME
WE CAN'T. AN ENEMY ARMY HAS ARRIVED. WE ARE THE ONES TRAPPED AND STARVING IN THE CITY NOW
OH, SNOTBALLS
THERE WAS ONLY ONE THING TO DO...
WHAT CAN WE DO?
RIDE OUT AND ATTACK THEM
IF SAINT GEORGE WAS HELPING, THEN WHY WASN'T HE AROUND WHEN THE PLAGUE STRUCK THE CRUSADERS IN ANTIOCH?
LET'S GET OUT OF THIS PLACE. LET'S HEAD FOR JERUSALEM
POKE
AGAIN THEY CAPTURED A CITY WITH NO FOOD. AGAIN THEY MASSACRED THE PEOPLE. A WRITER SAID...
The crusaders, excited by such a great victory,
rushed through the streets
and into the houses and mosques
killing all that they met,
men, women and children alike.
All that afternoon and all through the night
the massacre went on.
When Raymond of Aguilers went
to visit the temple the next morning
he had to pick his way through corpses
and blood that reached up to his knees.
BUT THIS TIME THEY DIDN'T WASTE THE CORPSES. A KNIGHT WROTE...
OUR TROOPS BOILED PAGAN ADULTS IN COOKING POTS, AND ROASTED CHILDREN ON SPITS AND ATE THEM GRILLED

A MAD MONK CALLED PETER BARTHOLOMEW SAID HE FOUND A HOLY SPEAR INSIDE THE CITY. IT WAS A MIRACLE, A GOOD LUCK CHARM FOR THE CRUSADERS.

ATTACK THE PAGANS! SPEAR TODAY, GONE TOMORROW

THE CRUSADERS RODE OUT WITH ONLY A HUNDRED FIT HORSES. THEY WOULD BE MASSACRED. THEN ANOTHER 'MIRACLE' OCCURRED...

OK! IN THE HILLS! AN ARMY OF MEN ON WHITE HORSES WITH WHITE BANNERS

IT'S SAINT GEORGE HIMSELF COMING TO RESCUE US. A GOLDEN OLDIE

HE'S BEEN DEAD 700 YEARS. HE'LL BE A GOLDEN MOULDY

THE CRUSADERS WON THE BATTLE. BUT WHO WERE THE MYSTERIOUS ARMY?

IT'S AN ARMY OF FRIENDS FROM TURKEY - NOT ST GEORGE AND NOT A MIRACLE

IT'S A MIRACLE THAT OUR FRIENDS ARRIVED AT JUST THE RIGHT TIME

THE CRUSADERS WROTE TO THE POPE TO SAY 'SORRY' FOR EATING PEOPLE.

I FORGIVE THEM. GOD SAYS IT IS ALL RIGHT TO EAT A PAGAN IF YOU ARE STARVING. WHICH REMINDS ME ... WHAT'S FOR DINNER?

A CRUSADER HAPPY MEAL ... PAGAN PUDDING WITH PEAS AND PARSNIPS

That victory at Jerusalem didn't do the Crusaders much good. The Turks fought back and defeated the First Crusade in the end. A Second Crusade set out to rescue the first lot. They failed. Then a Third Crusade, with England's King Richard the Lionheart, tried again. Richard was up against tough Turk Saladin and failed. Lots of Turks and Christians died horrible deaths but their deaths did not change anything. By 1291, not quite 200 years after the First Crusade, the Christians lost their last city in the Holy Land.

4

THE MINSTREL'S HORRIBLE HISTORY

The Tudors were a family of five kings and queens that ruled from 1485 till 1603. I wrote these little ditties so we can remember them ... just don't tell a Tudor or they may have me beheaded!

HENRY VII (reigned 1485–1509)

Claim to fame:
- after taking the crown from Richard III he made sure he kept it. He married Richard's niece, Elizabeth – a smart move which put his former enemies on his side. England was united after the long Wars of the Roses
- during Henry's reign two young men came forward and each claimed to be one of the Princes in the Tower, and the rightful king. Henry defeated both rebellions and kept a tight grip on the crown
- he also kept a tight grip on his money

Henry Tudor beat Richard the Thirder
When the battle turned into pure murder
He pinched Richard's crown
For the ride back to town
He was top man! He could go no further

HENRY VIII (reigned 1509-1547)

Claim to fame:
- got rid of the Catholic Church in England and made himself head of the new church. That gave him the chance to divorce his first wife and also to pinch the riches of the Catholic Church
- he built the first modern navy
- he liked hunting, eating, riding, eating, archery, eating, music, eating . . . and getting his own way. Anyone who annoyed him tended to get the chop - even a good friend like Thomas More

King Henry was fat as a boar
He'd had six wives and still wanted more
Anne and Kate said, "By heck!
He's a pain in the neck"
As their heads landed smack on the floor

EDWARD VI (reigned 1547-1553)

Claim to fame:
- aged nine when his father died and he came to the throne
- brought in the English Prayer book which caused a spot or two of bother
- the last thing he wanted was his Catholic sister Mary to get her bum on the throne. But he did the wrong thing . . . he carelessly died at the age of 15

At nine years the little king, Eddie
Had a grip on the throne quite unsteady
He was all skin and bone
Grown men fought for his throne
And by fifteen young Eddie was deddie

MARY I (reigned 1553-1558)

Claim to fame:
- married the King of Spain, then got England drawn into Spain's battles with France. Her unpopular marriage caused an English rebellion led by Thomas Wyatt. Wyatt lost the first battle and was executed
- fanatical Catholic, had Protestants burned at the stake if they didn't change back to her religion
- a sickly and unhappy woman who went down in history as "Bloody Mary" though she wasn't cruel in herself . . . just trying to do what she thought right

Bloody Mary they say was quite mad
And the nastiest taste that she had
Was for Protestant burning
It seems she had a yearning
To kill even more than her dad

ELIZABETH I (reigned 1558-1603)

Claim to fame:
- beat the Spanish Armada (with a little help from Francis Drake and the English navy)
- never married . . . though she had a few flings
- tried hard to stay young with harsh chemical make-up and hair dye so she ended up bald and toothless

A truly great queen was old Lizzie
She went charging around being busy
She thought herself beaut
But her teeth looked like soot
And her hair it was all red and frizzy

SPAIN GAINS
SIR FRANCIS DRAKE AND THE SPANISH ARMADA

WHEN SCARY MARY DIED, HER SISTER ELIZABETH TOOK THE THRONE. LIZZIE WAS THE LAST OF THE TERRIFYING TUDORS AND JUST AS AWFUL AS THE OTHERS. KING PHILIP OF SPAIN STILL FANCIED THE ENGLISH THRONE SO HE SET OFF WITH A MASSIVE FLEET OF SHIPS - THE ARMADA - TO INVADE. FRIZZY LIZZIE COULDN'T STOP HIM ALONE. SHE NEEDED THE HELP OF HER SUPER SAILORS. MEN LIKE SIR FRANCIS DRAKE...

SOMETHING FISHY THIS WAY COMES

THE EXPLORER

TUDOR SUPERHEROES WERE A BIT LIKE MODERN SUPERHEROES.

CAPE!

PANTS WORN ON OUTSIDE!

TIGHTS!

HORRIBLE HISTORIES NOT[E]
WE HAVE NO PROOF THAT DRA[KE] EVER USED HIS CAPE TO FLY.

DOUGHTY WAS ARRESTED AND SENT TO ONE OF THE SMALLEST SHIPS IN DRAKE'S FLEET. HE MOANED THAT HE HAD NO FOOD OR WATER. THE CREW TOLD HIM...

EEUW!

EAT AND DRINK FROM THE POO BUCKETS WE HAVE ON DECK

HONK HUM

NO. POO

DOUGHTY HAD TRIED TO LEAD A MUTINY AGAINST CAPTAIN DRAKE. THERE WAS ONLY ONE WAY TO DEAL WITH MUTINY...

CUT OFF HIS HEAD!

GIVE ME A BREAK, DRAKE

WITH DOUGHTY DEAD, DRAKE SAILED ON TO ROB SPANISH GALLEONS AND FINISH HIS VOYAGE AROUND THE WORLD. THE TREASURE HE SHARED WITH ELIZABETH WAS WORTH MILLIONS OF POUNDS...

AND I'LL MAKE YOU SIR FRANCIS DRAKE. YOU'VE MADE ME DAY...

SO YOU'LL MA[KE] ME KNIGHT? HEH! HEH!

2

STORM HELPED THE LUCKY DUCKY. IT DROVE THE SPANISH INTO THE SHALLOW WATERS NEAR HOLLAND. DRAKE WENT AFTER THEM...

SET FIRE TO SOME OLD SHIPS. LET THE WIND CARRY THEM INTO THE SPANISH FLEET

NOT A GOOD IDEA

THE INVASION WAS OVER. BUT, IN ENGLAND, QUEEN LIZ DIDN'T KNOW THAT. SHE WAITED WITH HER TROOPS. SHE WAS SUPPOSED TO HAVE MADE A FAMOUS SPEECH...

I may have the body of a weak and feeble woman, but I have the heart and stomach of a king.

I HOPE THE KING DOESN'T WANT THEM BACK!

LIKE THE BOWLS STORY, THIS WAS TOLD MANY YEARS LATER. MAYBE SHE NEVER SAID IT AT ALL.

A YEAR AFTER THE ARMADA WAS BEATEN...

NOW, DUCKY, I WANT YOU TO GO TO SPAIN AND SINK THE REST OF THEIR SHIPS

GREAT DRAKE WILL MAKE THE SPANISH SHAKE AND QUAKE

MANY SPANISH SHIPS BURNED, THE REST WERE SCATTERED.

Elizabeth didn't just want Spanish gold. She also discovered that selling African prisoners in America made her sailors a lot of money. Money that she shared. She had started the slave trade. It would bring misery to millions for over two hundred years. Drake was deadly, but the last Tudor queen was far more cruel. Drake had Doughty's head cut off. But Queen Liz had hundreds of people executed ... and one of them was her own cousin.

Mary executed her cousin too, remember. Seems to have been the Tudors' horrible hobby.

THE CAULD LAD'S LAMENT

Not all knights were gentlemen. In fact some were murderous bullies. In 1609 Lord Hylton of Hylton Castle (now in Sunderland) caught a stable lad, Robin Skelton, asleep. He took a horse whip and beat and kicked the boy to teach him a lesson. But he killed him – so the boy didn't get much of a lesson. Lord Hylton tried to cover up his crime by throwing the boy's corpse into the castle pond. The ghostly boy rose from the pond and to this day he can be heard moaning,

"I'm cauld! So cauld." (That's "cold" to you posh people.)

Chorus:
I'm cauld, I'm cauld, I'm so cauld,
I'm slimy and clammy as a lump of lard.
If you work for Hylton be on your guard,
He hits you with a whip and he hits you hard.

1. I worked in the stable but I fell asleep
His lordship found me dozing in a big straw heap.
He whipped me and he kicked me till he made me weep
Then he chucked me into the pond so deep.

Chorus

2. My sad, sad tale is not a fable
I was a groom in the Hylton stable.
I worked just as hard as I was able ... of course
Alas I never said goodbye to Mabel ... the horse.

Chorus

3. If you go to Hylton then you'll be thrilled.
Go along there when the night air's stilled.
Old Hylton he did beat me till I was killed.
Listen hard and hear me moan, "I'm chilled!"

Chorus

Lord Hylton was sent for trial on the charge of murdering Robin Skelton. The judge was an old friend of Lord Hylton and found the murderer "Not guilty" - one law for the rich, another for the poor. So poor Robin never got justice and that's why he can never rest in peace.

SPOT THE LOT
Can you spot all 8 differences?

REMEMBER, REMEMBER...

Since the Gunpowder Plot was discovered it has passed into English history and is remembered every 5 November. But how many of these funny Fawkes facts are false? Answers on page 57.

1 In January 1606 Parliament passed a new law. It said that 5 November would become a holiday of public thanksgiving.

2 Guy Fawkes hasn't always been the one on top of bonfires. At different times in history dummies of different people have been burned on 5 November.

3 It wasn't until 1920 that fireworks were added to the 5 November celebrations.

4 For many years the people of Scotton village in Yorkshire refused to celebrate 5 November with fireworks and bonfires.

5 The government decided that the cellars beneath Parliament should be patrolled night and day to prevent another Gunpowder Plot. That patrol stopped a long time ago.

PENNY FOR THE GUY

TALK LIKE A STUART

Every age has its own slang. Are any of your schoolmates 'bagpipes' or 'barnacles?' (That's chatterboxes or hangers-on, of course.)

Why not amaze and impress your teacher/parent/gerbil by reciting this sad tale? They will certainly say, 'Well!/Gosh!/Eeeek!' ... and then ask you to explain.

The Fate of the Fustilugs

There once was a fustilugs[1] slabberdegullion[2]
Who grew up quite buffle[3], not dossy[4].
He learned how to mill-ben[5], to pug[6] and to dub[7]
Then this dunaker[8] jiggled[9] a hossy[10].

But at budging[11] a beak[12] he was such a fopdoodle[13]
He was caught and sent down to the clink[14].
'Oh the cage[15] belly-timber[16] is pannam[17] and old horse[18]
And we only get water to drink.'

[1] a dirty-eared child, [2] a slob, [3] stupid, [4] brainy, [5] break and enter houses, [6] steal, [7] pick locks, [8] animal thief, [9] rustled, [10] horse – all right, this is not a Stuart slang word – but you try finding something to rhyme with 'dossy', [11] dodging, [12] constable – later a judge, [13] useless person, [14] the name of a London prison, [15] prison, [16] food, [17] bread, [18] dried, salted beef

CHOP-CHOP! THE GUILLOTINE

The guillotine is best known for its use during the French Revolution. This speedy slicing machine could kill kings cleanly and queens quickly, and lop lords and ladies like lightning.

Foul guillotine facts

1 The first French guillotine was built by Dr Joseph Guillotin . . . but he had advice on how to build it. Who advised him? King Louis XVI. He probably regretted it when he was later executed by guillotine. What must he have been thinking as he laid his head on the machine?

2 Chopping French aristo heads started before the guillotines were built. The first day of the French Revolution was 14 July 1789. On that day one nobleman, the Marquis of Launay, the governor of the Bastille, was caught by a Paris mob who cut off his head with a knife. His followers suffered the same charming chopping and their heads were paraded around Paris. The guillotine didn't replace the knife for another three years.

3 The guillotine is a famous machine of the French Revolution . . . but head-chopping machines had been invented 200 years before. One was used in Halifax, northern England, to execute cattle thieves and one was used in Scotland when the Earl of Morton was executed on it in 1581. The Scots called it 'The Maiden'. Dr Guillotin pinched the English and Scottish idea.

4 The guillotine was quick, and good executioners could get through two victims a minute. Not easy.

5 The head shooting off from the guillotine became known as 'sneezing into the basket'. Atch-ouch. The guillotine itself was known as what?
a) The Red Theatre?
b) The People's Avenger?
c) The National Razor?
Answer: All three.

6 The guillotine was tested first on live sheep and calves, then on dead bodies. Finally it was tried out on a live highwayman called Pelletier. Crowds turned out on 25 April 1792 to watch his execution. They went away grumbling, 'It was all over so quickly. It was no fun at all.' They marched off singing. . .

7 The French Revolution Terror from 1792 to 1794 sliced lots of heads off in two years – but the St Bartholomew's Day Massacre in 1572 killed more in one DAY.

8 One woman made a living by making wax masks from the dead heads in the guillotine basket. Her name was Madame Tussaud. Nice job.

9 Dr Guillotin invented the guillotine because he was such a kind man! He didn't want criminals to suffer. He said all they'd feel would be a tickle at the back of the neck. Oh yeah? Care to try it and prove it? One victim who felt nothing was called Valaze. He stabbed himself to death in court in 1793 – but the judge said his corpse had to be guillotined anyway.

10 Some French doctors took a front seat at the executions to test if the head lived on after the chop. When the head fell they called out the victim's name. One reported...

WHEN I CALLED OUT THE NAME THE EYES OPENED AND THEY STAYED LOOKING AT ME FOR THIRTY SECONDS.

That's nonsense (you'll be pleased to know if you are ever sent to the guillotine).

Happy ending 1?

It's said Dr Guillotin's cousin, also called Guillotin, helped him to design the killing machine. But then he had to watch as the woman he loved lost her head on their invention. Cousin Guillotin turned against the executioners and worked for their enemies – the people who wanted a King of France again. This was treason – Cousin Guillotin was arrested and executed. How? With the guillotine, of course.

Happy ending 2?

France's chief guillotine executioner was Charles-Henri Sanson. He was good at his job and once executed 300 men and women in three days. He wasn't keen on executing women and he did not enjoy executing King Louis XVI – but he didn't dare refuse.

It was a tricky job, high up on the blood-soaked platform. One day Charles-Henri's son, Gabriel, was helping Dad to deadhead the traitors. Gabriel slipped, fell off the platform and crashed to the cobbled street below. Gabriel died. After that a fence was put up round the guillotine platform. The last public execution on a guillotine was in 1939.

I HEARD THAT!

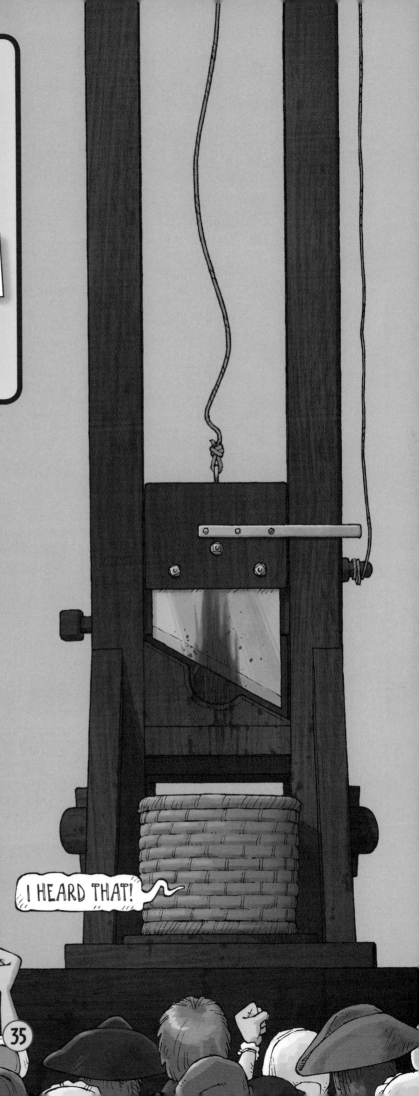

GRUESOME GAGS!

YUMMY!

WOW!

UUURGHH!

PUTRID PRIZES

Three lucky readers will each win a putrid prize pack including tickets to *Groovy Greeks* and *Incredible Invaders* – the latest Horrible Histories touring shows from Birmingham Stage Company!

We all want to meet people from history – the trouble is everyone is dead! So it's time to prepare yourselves for Groovy Greeks and Incredible Invaders ... live on stage! Using actors and amazing new 3D video effects, these two astounding new shows are guaranteed to thrill you and your children. Historical figures and events from the Greek, Roman, Saxon and Viking periods will come alive on stage and hover at your fingertips! (Find out more at: www.birminghamstage.com)

The three lucky winners will also receive a host of Horrible Histories goodies, including an Awesome Art Set, a Vicious Vikings book, key ring and mug set plus a selection of Vicious Vikings stationery.

To be in with a chance of winning, simply send us your own Horrible Histories four-line rhyme or five-line limerick. Entries should be about any historical person or event you've read about in this Annual. The winning poems will be published in the *Horrible Histories Annual 2016*!

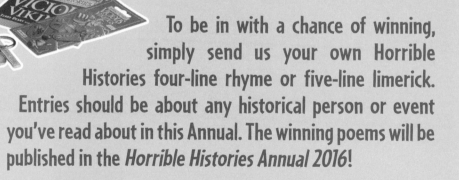

Send your entry to:

Horrible Histories Annual 2015 Competition
Scholastic Children's Books
Euston House
24 Eversholt Street
London
NW1 1DB

Don't forget to add your name, age, address and postcode to the back of the entry, so that we know where to send the prizes. Please get your parent or guardian to sign the back of your entry before you put it into an envelope.

The competition closes on 13th April 2015. Winning entrants will be notified within one month of the closing date.

Savage small-print

Send entries to: Horrible Histories Annual 2015 Competition, Scholastic Children's Books, Euston House, 24 Eversholt Street, London, NW1 1DB. Entrants must be under 18 years old 12 midnight British Summer Time on 13th April 2015, and must ask permission from a parent or guardian before entering. Entries are only valid if they include an original poem, your name and address. The three prize-winners automatically accept that Scholastic Children's Books will be using their address to notify them of their prize. One entry per person only. All entries will be entered into the competition. The three winners will be chosen by the judges after the closing date. The judges' decision is final and no correspondence will be entered into. All entries shall become the property and copyright of Scholastic Ltd. This competition is open to all Horrible Histories Annual 2015 (published by Scholastic Ltd) readers that are residents of the UK, Channel Islands and Isle of Man except employees of Scholastic UK, Birmingham Stage Company or anyone concerned with this promotion or to members of their immediate family. Each of the three prizes includes tickets for two children and two adults (one of whom must be a parent or guardian of one of the two children) to Groovy Greeks and Incredible Invaders, a Birmingham Stage Company production – winners will be notified of production dates and tickets will be allocated according to availability. The prize excludes transport, food and any costs of an overnight stay. The contents of the prize packs may include substitutions, depending on availability. The names of the winners may be shared with Birmingham Stage Company for the purposes of prize delivery. The prize winners may be requested to take part in a presentation, which may be used for publicity purposes. If in circumstances beyond our control we are unable to organize a prize, we will endeavour to organize an alternative prize of a similar value. No cash alternative will be offered. Entries must not be sent in through agents or third parties. Entries must not include poems believed to be copied. Any such entries will be invalid. The winners will be notified in writing within 28 days of the closing date. If an entry chosen to be a prize-winner does not include valid contact details or the prize-winner rejects the prize, Scholastic Ltd will draw a replacement prize-winner. The name and county of the winner will be made available on request and receipt of a SAE. Scholastic Ltd reserves the right to cancel the competition at any stage if deemed necessary, or if circumstances arise outside our control. Entrants will be deemed to have accepted these rules and agreed to be bound by them when entering the competition. No purchase is necessary. You can contact the promoter of the competition at Scholastic Children's Books, Euston House, 24 Eversholt Street, London, NW1 1DB. The competition closes at 12 midnight British Summer Time on 13th April 2015. No entries will be accepted after that date and no responsibility will be accepted for entries lost or damaged.

THE BIG VICTORIAN QUIZ

MEASLY MANNERS

If a time machine dropped your dad in 1800s London would he be a gentleman ... or a slob? Test him with these 'do' and 'don't' problems to see if he could have been accepted by polite Victorians. Just one problem ... if he makes a single mistake he could well be frowned on for the rest of his life!

A book of Gentlemen's Manners gave the advice ...

1 Do/Don't ... bite into your piece of bread.

2 Do/Don't ... call your servants "girls".

3 Do/Don't ... raise your hat to a lady in the street.

4 Do/Don't ... spit on the pavement.

5 Do/Don't ... sit with legs crossed.

6 Do/Don't ... offer your hand to an older person to be shaken.

7 Do/Don't ... eat from the side of your soup spoon and not the end.

8 Do/Don't ... write to people you know on postcards.

9 Do/Don't ... remove your overcoat before you enter someone's living room.

10 Do/Don't ... use slang words.

HOWZAT VICTORIA?

The English lost a cricket match against Australia for the first time in 1880. They burned a bail to ashes and have played for those Ashes ever since. "How's that?" the cricketers cried (or "Howzat?" in cricket language) when they thought a batsman was out. And "Howzat?" is the question about these curious Queen Victoria facts.

1 She was the shortest and the longest reigning monarch Britain ever had! Howzat?

2 Victoria was responsible for the death of her beloved husband, Albert. Howzat?

3 The police set Victoria up as the target for a murdering gunman. Howzat?

4 Victoria was highly respectable all her life yet she caused a scandal in her coffin. Howzat?

5 Albert and Victoria were married in 1840 though he never proposed to her. Howzat?

6 The Victorians liked portrait paintings but the Queen liked the portraits different. Howzat?

7 Victoria was Queen of England yet the 'Queen's English' was never very good. Howzat?

ODD ONE OUT

The 19th century was a time of great invention. There are fifteen inventions in this picture ... but only ten were first produced between 1800 and 1900, anywhere in the world. Can you spot the odd ones out and the odd ones in? See page 59 for the answers.

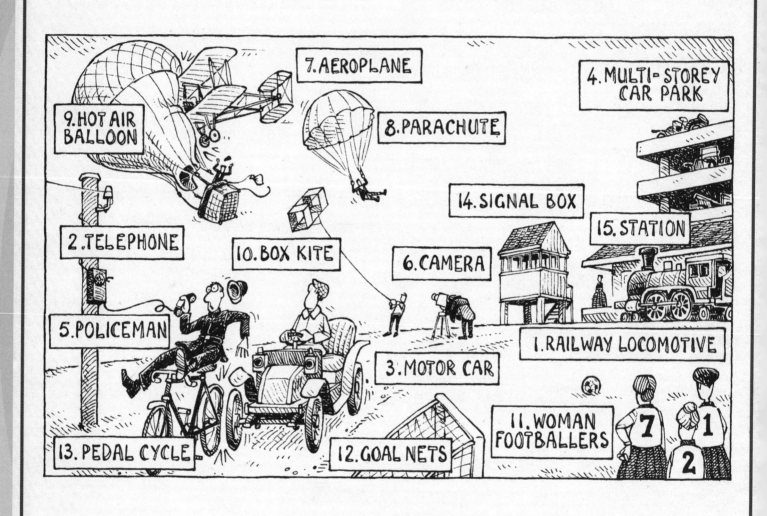

GRUESOME GARROTTERS

IN THE 1850S AND 1860S A NEW TERROR HIT THE CITY STREETS - GARROTTING. A VICTORIAN VILLAIN EXPLAINED TO OUR HORRIBLE HISTORIES REPORTER...

FIRST WORLD WAR FILES

FRIGHTFUL FIRST WORLD WAR TIMELINE

The war started in August 1914 and the soldiers were sure it would be a short sharp fight. 'One big battle and we'll win' ... each side said. 'It will be over by Christmas', the soldiers told each other. They didn't know there would be four killing Christmases before the fighting was finished. Four years of mud and blood and bullets and bombs and bitter, blinding gas. A war-weary world made a sort of peace in November 1918, and poppies and grass grew over the graves.

1914

28 June - Archduke Franz Ferdinand is assassinated in Bosnia. Austria is very annoyed because he was going to be their next emperor. (Franz is too dead to be annoyed.)

23 July - Austria blames Serbia for the death of Ferdi. Serbia grovels but apology is not accepted. This means WAR.

4 August - German army marches through Belgium to attack France, so Britain joins the war to help 'poor little Belgium'.

30 August - Meanwhile, in the east, the German army defeats the Russian army. Round one to Germany.

9 September - The French stop the Germans at the Battle of the Marne. Round two to France.

22 November - The two sides have battered one another to a standstill in northern France. They dig 'trenches' opposite one another ... and won't move from them much for four years.

25 December - Enemies stop fighting for a day or two, and even play friendly football matches.

1915

19 January - First Zeppelin airship bombing raids on Britain.

4 February - Germany says it will surround Britain with submarines, sink food supply ships and starve Britain to defeat.

March - British Government asks women to sign up for war work. Many do and they start doing it better than the men did!

22 April - Nasty new weapon, poisoned gas, first used against soldiers in the trenches.

7 May - German submarines sink a passenger ship, the Lusitania - on board are 128 Americans who are not even part of the war yet. Big mistake, Germany.

July - The Turkish state uses war as an excuse to wipe out an entire race of people, the Armenians. A step on the road to the terrors of the Second World War.

August - Food getting short, especially in Germany. Prices go up and taxes go up to pay for the war - £1 million a day in Britain is needed to pay for the fighting.

12 October - Nurse Edith Cavell is caught helping Brit prisoners to escape in Belgium. She says, 'If I had to, I'd do it all over again.' Germans shoot her so she can't.

1916

25 January - 'Conscription' comes to Britain. That means fit, single men have to join the army whether they like it or not.

February – The French and Germans begin the longest battle of the war, at the fortress of Verdun in north-eastern France. Even Big Bertha (that's a gun firing one-ton shells, not a woman) can't win it for the Germans.

March – German soldiers are told to have one day a week without food to save on supplies ... but the officers seem to eat well every day!

31 May – The only great sea battle of the war takes place at Jutland. Germans claim victory but never try to fight the Brit navy again.

1 July – The Battle of the Somme begins. Today Brits outnumber Germans seven to one ... but lose seven men to every one German. Very bloody draw.

10 August – A frightful news film, The Battle of the Somme, is shown in Brit cinemas even though it's not over yet. It's seen by 20 million shocked Brits.

15 September – New Brit super-weapon, the 'Willie', enters the war. Luckily someone has changed its name to the 'Tank'.

18 November – End of the Battle of the Somme.

1917

January – A munitions factory blows up in Silvertown, East London, killing 73.

February – The Russian people rebel against their leaders and Russian soldiers lend their rifles to help the revolution. Good news for Germany.

April – The Doughboys are here! No, not bakers' men, but American soldiers as the USA joins the war. Meanwhile French troops rebel against their conditions.

June – Brit ban on rice being thrown at weddings and feeding birds – food is too precious.

July – The war now costs Britain nearly £6 million a day. Will they run out of money or men first?

1 August – Terrific rain storms as the British attack in Flanders. The mud is as deadly an enemy as the Germans.

September – German submarines shell Scarborough.

October – Brit bakers allowed to add potato flour to bread while French bread has become grey, soggy stuff.

6 December – German Giants reach London. (They're bomber aircraft, not monster men.) They're harder to catch than the old Zeppelins.

1918

January – Britain is forced to have two meatless days a week and no meat for breakfast. Shops with margarine are raided by desperate women!

21 March – Called the 'last day of trench warfare'. The Germans break out and smash the Allies back from the trenches.

1 April – The Royal Air Force is formed and celebrate by shooting down German ace von Richthofen – the Red Baron – three weeks later.

June – 30 people die in Lancashire. They had Spanish flu. No one has any idea how many millions it's about to kill. Far more than the war, for sure.

July – At the Marne River the Allies stop retreating. The tide is turning back towards Germany. The Russian rebels massacre their royal family.

8 August – German General Ludendorff calls this 'the black day of the German army' as they are driven back. Still, no one expects the war to end this year.

October – German sailors are ordered to make one great last voyage to destroy the Brit fleet – or be destroyed. Sailors refuse and pour water on their ships' boiler fires.

9 November – Kaiser Wilhelm is thrown out of Germany. He retires to Belgium. After what he did to them four years ago it's not surprising they don't want him! He ends up in Holland.

11 November – Armistice Day and peace is agreed at last. The peace document is signed at the 11th hour of this 11th day of the 11th month.

LEARN THE LINGO

Every soldier needs to talk soldier language. Learn these and your sergeant will test you on them tomorrow!

ALLEY Go! Clear out! Run away! From French 'allez'.

BUMF Toilet paper, or newspaper used for the toilet. Later on it came to mean any useless letters from the army. From bum-fodder, a 1700s word.

CANTEEN MEDALS Beer or food stains on the front of your tunic.

CHARPOY Bed. From the Hindustani word.

CHAT A louse.

CHINSTRAPPED Tired, exhausted. The idea is a man can be so tired he is held upright only by the chinstrap of his cap or helmet. (It's a joke.) In fact chinstraps are used only by troops on horseback. Other soldiers think that if a bullet hits their helmet, the chinstrap may choke them or break their jaw.

COLD MEAT TICKET A disc worn around the neck. Men are given red and green discs. These give the name and number of the soldier. If he is killed, one disc stays with the body (the cold meat).

DAISIES Boots. From Cockney rhyming slang 'daisy roots'.

DEVIL DODGER Army priest.

FLEABAG Sleeping bag.

GOGGLE-EYED BOOGER WITH THE TIT British gas helmet. The wearer has to breathe in through his nose and breathe out through a valve held in his teeth.

JAKES Latrines. Expression dating back to Elizabethan times.

KILTIE A Scottish soldier.

KNUT A person (usually an officer) who is fussy about how they look. The word comes from the popular music-hall song by Arthur Wimperis (1874-1953) Gilbert the Filbert, the Colonel of the Knuts.

LANDOWNER A dead man. To 'become a landowner' was to be dead and buried.

QUICK FIRER A postcard. The card has sentences printed which can be crossed out to give your message. E.g. 'I am/ am not fit/dead and hope to be home soon/next year/in a box'.

RATS AFTER MOULDY CHEESE (RAMC) Doctors and nurses ... the Royal Army Medical Corps.

REST CAMP A cemetery.

THIRD MAN To go too far into danger. This is from a story that an enemy sniper can see a match struck at night. Light a second man's cigarette after your own and the sniper has time to take aim ... light the third man's and the sniper fires. The second man is fine – the third man is one too far.

ENEMY GENERALS

HOW TO DRAW A TRENCH RAT

Copy the Trench Rat into the squares.

Terrible Trench Toilets

The British dig trenches in the ground so they are safe from enemy bullets and can attack. The enemy sit in their trenches to defend. The French and British build simple trenches because they don't plan to stay there. They are always wanting to attack. The Germans build solid and clever trenches. They use concrete and have dugouts deep underground.

There are no proper toilets in most of the Brit trenches, just buckets. If you upset the sergeant then you may be given the job of taking the buckets out after dark. Your job is to dig a hole and empty the buckets.

DID YOU KNOW?
A soldier usually makes over a kilo of poo and pee each day. In an army company in the trenches this is a ton a week.

NAME THAT WEAPON

If you are going into battle you will need to carry a lot of stuff. The army gives you weapons (usually a bayonet and a rifle) but many soldiers use extra special ones too...

BAYONET

A long knife fastened to the end of your rifle. Used to stab the enemy to death when you haven't time to fire. Invented in France in the 1600s.
For: Good for toasting bread, opening cans, scraping mud off uniforms, poking a trench fire or digging toilet pits.
Against: You can have someone's eye out if you're not careful. And if you stick it in the enemy you may have trouble pulling it out again!

KNUCKLEDUSTERS

Wrap these around your fingers.
For: If you are hand-to-hand with a German soldier, and you have run out of bullets, these will help you smash his teeth in or put out his eyes ... if he doesn't get you first!
Against: Another heavy thing to carry and not much good if your enemy still has a loaded gun.

MAXIM MACHINE GUN

A gun that fires off a stream of bullets, around 10 bullets every second.
For: One machine gun is said to be worth around 80 rifles. Good for defending your trench.
Against: The Maxim weighs 62kg and needs to rest on a stand. It gets hot very quickly and bullets can jam. The British army is not keen on them in 1914 and only have a few hundred. The Germans have 12,000 at the start of the War and 100,000 by the end.

HAND GRENADE

Hand grenades are bombs you can throw – but in the First World War they can be deadly ... for the thrower! There are accidents every day.
For: They are thrown by hand...
Against: ...but you can only throw them about 30 metres. At 30 metres your enemy can shoot you. Oh, dear. So some soldiers invent grenades with handles. The hair brush (or racket) grenade was a paddle-shaped piece of wood with a tin box fastened to it. Steel plates in the box are flung out when it explodes and rip into enemy bodies and faces.

It's a bit hard to get the throwing right. Some soldiers have catapults. Elastic Y-shaped ones (like they used at school).

A sports shop in London, Gamages, makes one that fires grenades 150 metres. Sadly the rubber soon goes rotten. If it snaps as you let go the grenade lands at your feet. Oooops!

SPRING GUN

Captain West invents the spring gun. It is a cross between the Roman ballista and the medieval French trebuchet.

For: Can throw bombs up to 250 metres. It's still as dangerous as the hand-held ones.

Against: It has to be carried through the trenches by two men and if it fails then the bomb drops at your own feet.

SHARP SPADE

Many soldiers use a short-handled spade (or 'entrenching tool') fastened to their bayonet.

For: You can sharpen the blade so that it's just as deadly as a bayonet. These tools could then be used to 'dig in' after soldiers had taken a trench.

Against: Very clumsy to carry. It can trip you up or get caught in the barbed wire.

TANKS

These machines can move forward through mud. The soldiers on foot can walk behind and shelter from enemy bullets.

For: Good shields. Scare the enemy who often run away when they see them.

Against: They break down, and get stuck in the mud. Worst of all is if you're trapped inside when they catch fire.

CRICKET BALL GRENADE

A little bomb like a cricket ball with a handle. Strike the ball like a match then throw it.

For: Some other grenades explode at your feet if you drop them, but not this one. The Germans aren't very good at cricket so they can't bat it back.

Against: If the ball or the box get wet they won't work. If you can't throw a cricket ball you're not much use throwing this!

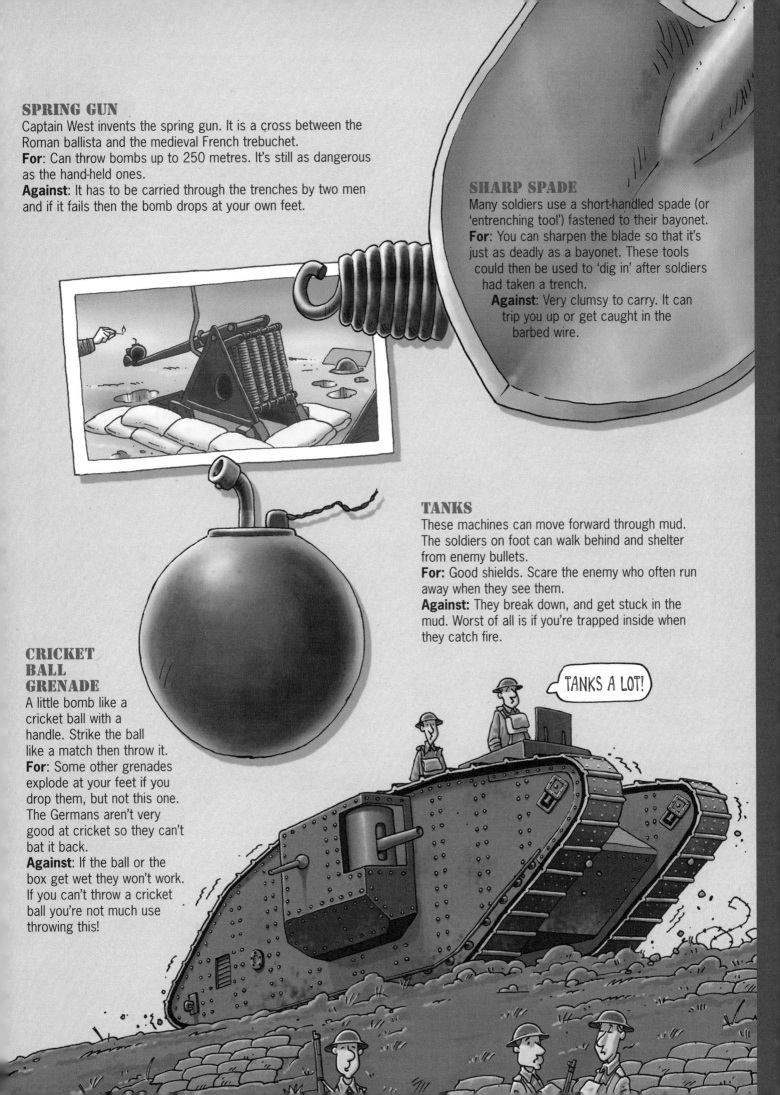

TANKS A LOT!

LIFE ON THE
HOME FRONT

DAFT DORA

Who was DORA? DORA was Britain's Defence of the Realm Act.
And DORA could be very fussy.
The people of Britain had to live by DORA's rules. But
which rules? Here are some strange regulations. But which
are real DORA rules and which are real daft rules?

DEFENCE OF THE REALM ACT

YOU MUST NOT

1 … loiter under a railway bridge
2 … send a letter overseas written in invisible ink
3 … buy binoculars without official permission
4 … fly a kite that could be used for signalling
5 … speak a foreign language on the telephone
6 … ring church bells after sundown
7 … whistle in the street after 10pm for a taxi
8 … travel alone in a railway carriage over the
Forth Bridge
9 … push a handcart through the streets
at night without showing a red light at
the back and a white light on the front
10 … eat sweets in the classroom

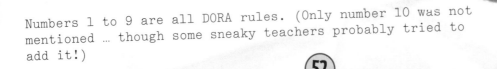

Numbers 1 to 9 are all DORA rules. (Only number 10 was not
mentioned … though some sneaky teachers probably tried to
add it!)

ZEPPELINS

A Zeppelin is a gas-filled balloon with a motor to take it where you want to go.

On 19 January 1915 the Germans make the first Zeppelin airship raids to drop bombs on Britain – on Great Yarmouth and Kings Lynn on the east coast. On 7 June 1915 the first Zeppelin airship is shot down over Flanders, northern France.

For: They can drop firebombs from a few hundred metres up, and kill over 500 people during the War. They can't aim well so this includes women and children, cats and dogs.

Against: That slow-moving bag of gas makes a Zeppelin an easy target for an enemy fighter plane. And they burn fiercely.

DID YOU KNOW...?

A Zeppelin is shot down over London and a reporter goes to see where it has crashed in flames. He writes ...

The crew numbered nineteen. One body was found in the field some way from the wreckage. He must have jumped from the doomed airship from a great height. So great was the force with which he struck the ground that I saw the print of his body clearly in the grass. There was a round hole for the head, then deep marks of the body, with outstretched arms, and finally the legs wide apart. Life was in him when he was picked up, but the spark soon went out. He was, in fact, the commander of the airship.

AWESOME ANSWERS

The Unusual Suspects page 12

Measly Middle Ages

Terrifying Tudors

Savage Stone Age

Gorgeous Georgians

Awful Egyptians

Rotten Romans

Spot the Lot page 14

IT'S THE ELEPHANT OF SURPRISE

Spot the Lot page 28

Remember, remember... page 32

1. True. People lit bonfires to celebrate and threw dummies on the fire dressed as Guy Fawkes.

2. True. The first record of this was at Cliffe Hill in London 1606 where a dummy of the Pope joined Guy Fawkes in the flames.

3. False. Within a few years of the plot people began to use fireworks on November 5.

4. True. This village was where Guy Fawkes used to live and the people didn't think it was fair that Guy should take all the blame.

5. False. A search of the cellars is still carried out before the opening of every Parliament.

Measly Manners page 40

1. Don't bite bread. Break off a piece and place it in your mouth.

2. Don't call servants "girls". Call them maids or servants.

3. Do raise your hat to a lady friend. BUT . . . wait till she has bowed to you first and do not wave your hat in the air the way the French do. Put it straight back onto your head. If she offers to shake hands then you may do so. If you are smoking then take your cigar out of your mouth with one hand as you raise your hat with the other.

4. Don't spit on the pavement . . . or anywhere else for that matter!

5. Don't sit with your legs crossed. The book admits that most men do this but says it is extremely impolite.

6. Don't offer your hand to an older person. Wait until they have offered it to you.

7. Do eat from the side of your soup spoon – and remember you mustn't gurgle or suck in your breath while you sip your soup.

8. Don't use postcards. Write letters or nothing at all.

9. Do remove your overcoat when entering someone's living room . . . even if you are only making a very short call.

10. Don't use slang words . . . usually. There are some slang words that a gentleman may use. If you don't know what they are then avoid slang altogether.

Howzat Victoria? page 41

1. She was the shortest in height but the longest in the time she spent on the throne.

2. The dirty water from her toilet leaked into Albert's drinking water and gave him the disease that killed him.

3. The gunman tried to shoot her as she drove in her carriage in London. His gun misfired and he escaped. The police told her to drive in the same place and at the same time the next day so that he could try again. He did! They caught him.

4. She was buried with a photograph of her "friend", her Scottish servant. In her hand was a lock of his hair. What had they been up to when she was alive, people wanted to know!

5. Victoria proposed to him!

6. Victoria (and hubby Albert) preferred the people in the pictures to have no clothes on!

7. She was from the German Hanover family so she always spoke with a German accent.

Odd One Out page 42

1. Railway locomotive – IN-vented in 1804 by Richard Trevithick. The Victorian age was the age of the railways with steam trains crossing the country. The first railway death was in 1828, when driver John Gillespie's boiler blew up on the famous Stockton and Darlington railway.

2. Telephone – IN-vented in 1876. US inventor Alexander Graham Bell usually gets the credit for this. (Although Johann Reis of Germany did show a telephone device in 1860 made of a violin case and a sausage skin!)

3. Motor car – IN-vented in France in 1862. The 19th century also saw the first road death (London, 1896), drunken driver (London, 1897), car theft (Paris, 1896) and speeding motorist (Kent, 1896).

4. Multi-storey car park - OUT... but only just. In May 1901 an electric carriage company built a 7-storey garage for its vehicles.

5. Policeman – OUT. The London police force was created in 1829 but the world's first was in Paris in 1667.

6. Camera – IN-vented in the 1830s.

7. Aeroplane – OUT. Orville Wright made the first powered heavier-than-air flight in 1903.

8. Parachute – OUT because the first jump was made from a hot-air balloon in 1797. You can be excused for getting this one wrong because the first jump in Britain was in 1802 and the first jump by a British person (who lived) was in 1838. The year before a Brit died trying.

9. Hot-air balloon – OUT. First flight made in 1783 near Paris.

10. Box kite – IN-vented in Australia, 1893.

11. Woman footballers – IN-vented in 1895 by Lady Florence Dixie who formed the British Women's Football Club.

12. Goal nets – IN-vented by a Liverpool engineer in 1890.

13. Pedal cycle – IN-vented in Scotland in 1839.

14. Signal box – IN-vented in London, 1839.

15. Station – IN-vented in Baltimore, USA in 1830.

WELL DONE

HORRIBLE HISTORIES
New Edition
MEASLY MIDDLE AGES
Splats, hats and lots of RATS!
Terry Deary
Illustrated by Martin Brown

HORRIBLE HISTORIES
New Edition
CUT-THROAT CELTS
Splats, hats and lots of RATS!
Terry Deary
Illustrated by Martin Brown

HORRIBLE HISTORIES
New Edition
SAVAGE STONE AGE
Splats, hats and lots of RATS!
Terry Deary
Illustrated by Martin Brown

HORRIBLE HISTORIES
THE BEASTLY BEST BITS
I NEVER FORGET A FACE!
Terry Deary Illustrated By Martin Brown

HORRIBLE HISTORIES
SPIES
WARNING: WWII SECRET AGENTS INSIDE
TERRY DEARY

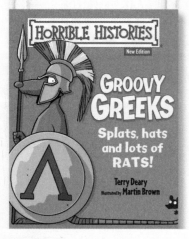

HORRIBLE HISTORIES
New Edition
GROOVY GREEKS
Splats, hats and lots of RATS!
Terry Deary
Illustrated by Martin Brown

HORRIBLE HISTORIES
New Edition
FRIGHTFUL FIRST WORLD WAR
Splats, hats and lots of RATS!
Terry Deary
Illustrated by Martin Brown

HORRIBLE HISTORIES
New Edition
VILE VICTORIANS
Splats, hats and lots of RATS!
Terry Deary
Illustrated by Martin Brown

HORRIBLE HISTORIES
New Edition
WOEFUL SECOND WORLD WAR
Splats, hats and lots of RATS!
Terry Deary
Illustrated by Martin Brown

HORRIBLE HISTORIES
New Edition
AWFUL EGYPTIANS
Splats, hats and lots of RATS!
Terry Deary
Illustrated by Martin Brown

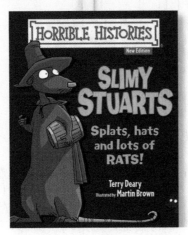

HORRIBLE HISTORIES
New Edition
SLIMY STUARTS
Splats, hats and lots of RATS!
Terry Deary
Illustrated by Martin Brown

HORRIBLE HISTORIES
New Edition
ROTTEN ROMANS
Splats, hats and lots of RATS!
Terry Deary
Illustrated by Martin Brown

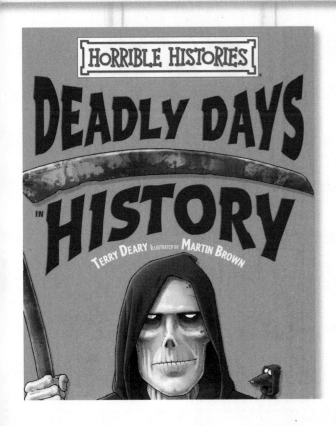

HORRIBLE HISTORIES
DEADLY DAYS in HISTORY
TERRY DEARY ILLUSTRATED BY MARTIN BROWN

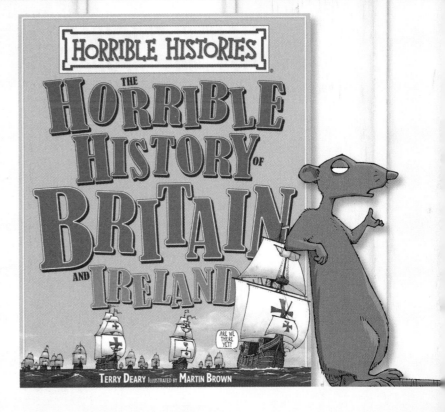

HORRIBLE HISTORIES
THE HORRIBLE HISTORY OF BRITAIN AND IRELAND
ARE WE THERE YET?
TERRY DEARY ILLUSTRATED BY MARTIN BROWN

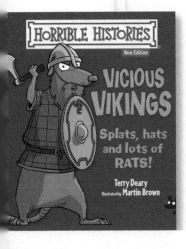

HORRIBLE HISTORIES
New Edition
VICIOUS VIKINGS
Splats, hats and lots of RATS!
Terry Deary
Illustrated by Martin Brown

HORRIBLE HISTORIES
New Edition
TERRIFYING TUDORS
Splats, hats and lots of RATS!
Terry Deary
Illustrated by Martin Brown

HORRIBLE HISTORIES
New Edition
SMASHING SAXONS
Splats, hats and lots of RATS!
Terry Deary
Illustrated by Martin Brown

COMING SOON

THE BIG FAT CHRISTMAS BOOK